Sheree Rose Kelley's

Breads & Spreads

To: Shawn,
Happy baking!

Cheers,
Sheree

THE NAUTILUS PUBLISHING COMPANY
Oxford, Mississippi

Published under contract with The Nautilus Publishing Company, 426 South Lamar Blvd., Suite 16, Oxford, Mississippi 38655, Tel: 662-513-0159, www.nautiluspublishing.com

First Edition

ISBN: 9781936946266

Photography by Michael Gomez
Editorial consultant, Roben Mounger
Food design by Amanda Alberto
Art Direction by The Nautilus Publishing Company

Library of Congress Cataloging-in-Publication Data has been applied for.

PRINTED IN CHINA
through a partnership with Four Colour Imprints, Louisville, Kentucky

10   9   8   7   6   5   4   3   2   1

"Do not forget to show hospitality to strangers, for by so doing some people have shown hospitality to angels without knowing it."

Hebrews 13:2

To Grandmommie

For all the Saturdays of lessons cooking, baking, canning, gardening and sewing.
For the Sundays of family and friends around the dinner table.
Your love and knowledge to never be forgotten.

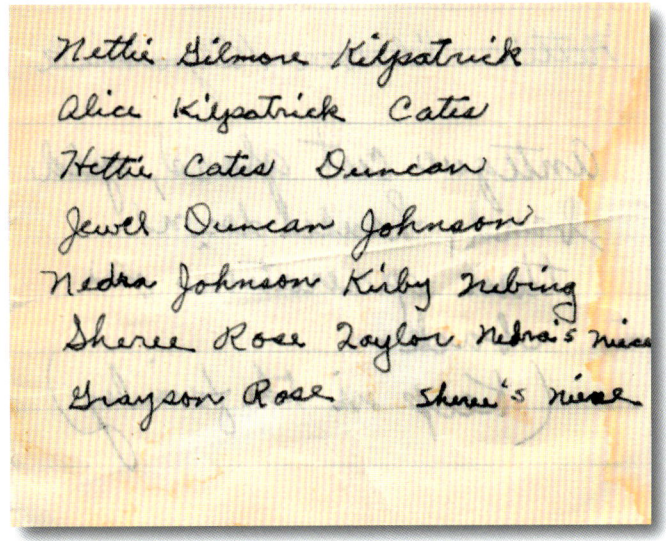

Left: Antique cut glass with gold band
Above: List of family members to whom vase has been passed down through generations

Breads & Spreads

Breads

Biscuits

Appetizers

Cornbread

Rolls

Specialties

Spreads & Gravies

Picking the Seasons

*N*o excuse.

Being from an endless line of great cooks and bakers, I have not a single reason — with the knowledge given me — not to use it all and pass it around.

Now comes the time for measuring out the particulars of a culinary education. Here, I am compelled to discuss Mama's Hushpuppies and Zesty Cocktail Sauce . . . and, there, to explain why Date Nut Bread and Orange Cream Cheese Spread are the perfect addition to baby and wedding showers. Hence, *Breads & Spreads*.

My desire to compile a cookbook of family recipes and ever-evolving discoveries comes from a love of good food, a fascination with stories, and a commitment to a delicious table spread for family and friends.

This book embraces our rural traditions and our metropolitan range.

My love of the country life starts with the ease of picking the seasons in Daddy's Pulaski garden. When he calls me with "the cherries are ready," I know that a trip to his garden will lead to the most scrumptious jam.

My love of the city ranges from sampling new restaurants to shopping for exotic ingredients.

I give nods to my Giles County roots and my Nashville wings.

● ● ●

I am grateful for all that Mama and Grandmommie passed along to me.

Now it's my great honor and pleasure to share it with you.

Tools

STAINLESS STEEL SCOOPS
Uniformity in measurement. Small: cookies, cheese crisps, hushpuppies, mini muffins. Medium: cookies, hot water cornbread, pancakes, creme puffs and hoe cakes. Large: muffins, spoon rolls, pop-overs.

WONDER CUP
Accurate for measuring dry/solid or liquid ingredients. Unique in its ability to measure and eject with a plunger all ingredients, especially sticky ones.

SIFTER
All flour and added spices should be sifted to create the lightest version of a recipe.

PLAIN OR SERRATED?
A serrated knife is always used in cutting bread and in the case of pinwheels and cinnamon rolls.

BISCUIT CUTTERS
An assortment of sizes is desirable, and depending on the occasion, small for appetizers and larger for meals is ideal.

Linen Napkins

Fine linens are a great love of mine. During our travels, I curated a wonderful assortment of antique Irish tablecloths as well as napkins. By haunting estate sales, I unearthed prized cocktail and dinner napkins. So if you come to our house for dinner, expect to use the "real" thing.

Mama Chef: Helpful Hints

On Mother's Day, 1995, my boys surprised me with a gift — Mama Chef. Throughout the book, Mama Chef will appear to offer helpful hints. Just like she reminds me, on ocassion, of something I shouldn't forget.

Breads

Harvest Pumpkin Bread

*G*randmommie always used the freshly grown pumpkin from Grandaddy's patch to make her pumpkin bread.

My family would harvest the pumpkins from his patch. We loaded a trailer with those beauties and into Pulaski we would go so my boys could sell: small, 50¢ - medium, $1 - large, $2.

I enjoy making pumpkin bread a seasonal event. For me there is nothing like that pumpkin spice smell floating through the house.

At the first hint of fall, I bring this recipe out and make this bread during the entire holiday season.

See three recipes next page

Pumpkin Bread

3 ½ cups flour
2 teaspoons baking soda
1 ½ teaspoons salt
1 teaspoon cinnamon
1 teaspoon nutmeg
3 cups sugar
4 eggs
1 cup oil
2/3 cup orange juice
1 (15 ounce) can of pure pumpkin or 2 cups of
   baked pumpkin
1 teaspoon vanilla extract
1/2 cup golden raisins
1/2 cup dried cranberries
1/2 cup chopped pecans (optional)

- Preheat oven to 350 degrees.
- Grease bottom and sides and then sift flour to completely coat the grease (knock off excess flour) of two 9 x 5 inch loaf pans.
- In a smaller mixing bowl, combine flour, baking soda, salt, cinnamon and nutmeg.
- In a larger mixing bowl, combine sugar, pumpkin, eggs, oil, vanilla and orange juice until just blended.
- Add flour mixture to pumpkin mixture, beat just until moistened. Stir in raisins, cranberries and pecans.
- Divide mixture between the two prepared loaf pans.
- Bake for 1 hour or until a toothpick inserted in the center comes out clean.
- Cool in pans for 10 minutes then remove to wire racks to complete cooling.

I often make these in four small stoneware loaf pans. Bake for 45 to 50 minutes. Cool as above. Place on paper doily and into small cellophane bags with ribbon for a hostess gift.

Grandmommie's Baked Pumpkin

• Preheat the oven to 400 degrees.
• Wash the pumpkin in warm water and then dry.
• Slice the stem off. Cut the pumpkin in half. Scrap out seeds and strings.
• Save seeds to roast.
• Drizzle pumpkin with melted butter.
• Place cut side down on a baking sheet.
• Roast about 40 to 45 minutes.
• Prick with fork to make sure it is very soft.
• Cool pumpkin for 10 minutes or until ready to handle.
• Peel and place in food processor to make pumpkin puree.
• Pulse until no clumps are left.

Roasted Pumpkin Seeds

1 cup raw pumpkin seeds
2 teaspoons butter, melted
1/2 teaspoon sea salt

• Preheat oven to 325 degrees.
• Wash and drain seeds in a colander and lightly dry with a paper towel.
• Toss seeds in bowl with melted butter and salt. Stir to coat.
• Spread the seeds in a single layer on a parchment paper lined baking sheet and bake for 10 minutes.
• Remove from the oven and stir.
• Roast another 10 minutes. During the last 5 minutes of roasting, remove a few seeds and crack open to make sure the inner seeds are not burning. The inner seed should have only a hint of golden tinge to it. They should not be brown.
• When ready, remove the seeds from the oven.

No need to remove the outer shell.
I love pumpkin seeds and they are so, so good for you!

Big Mama's Muffins

My son Blake's Great Grandmother Mary Britton was known to everyone as Big Mama. She was a wonderful cook and always wore an apron. She worked the restaurant inside Kuhn's Department Store on the square in Pulaski. Kuhn's space was large and its restaurant was in the back of the store. I loved the store basement where all the toys were displayed.

These bran muffins were a treat that she enjoyed sending to friends and family. The recipe produces about a total of 60 muffins and any unbaked batter can be stored in the refrigerator for up to one week.

I have provided the substitutions for something a bit healthier but, some things are best left as is and you can cut your calories somewhere else…maybe walk a few more miles.

20 ounce box Raisin Bran
1 quart buttermilk
4 cups of sugar (or 2 cups of sugar and 1 ½ cup honey)
5 cups self-rising flour (or 4 cups of self-rising flour and
**   1 cup whole wheat)**
2 teaspoons baking soda
4 eggs, well beaten
1 cup vegetable oil (or 1 ½ cups applesauce)
2 teaspoons vanilla extract
1 cup golden raisins

- Preheat the oven to 350 degrees.
- Mix ingredients as they are listed in a large bowl.
- Fill 3/4 full the cups in a greased muffin pan
  (use large stainless steel scoop).
- Bake for 20 to 25 minutes or until golden brown.

Date Nut Bread

As long as I can remember, a joy in my life has been to attend and serve as host for both baby and wedding showers. The Date Nut Bread and Orange Cream Cheese Spread are perfect examples of what I best loved to prepare for these occasions throughout the years.

My dear friend, Jane Higgins, was expecting her first baby during the winter of 1985. Jane was ordered bedrest and was unable to attend the baby shower that our Sunday school class planned for her.

So on a cold and snowy Sunday afternoon, with presents, cake, punch, mints, breads and spreads in tow; we carried the party to her. I will never forget her sweet little angel Ellen who was born into this world shortly afterwards.

Date Nut Bread

2 cups dates, chopped
1 cup hot tea
1/4 cup unsalted butter, softened
3/4 cup light brown sugar, packed
1 large egg, slightly beaten
1 cup whole wheat flour
3/4 cup all-purpose flour
2 teaspoons baking powder
1 teaspoon baking soda
3/4 teaspoon sea salt crystals
1/2 teaspoon cinnamon
1/4 teaspoon nutmeg
1/4 teaspoon ginger
1 teaspoon vanilla extract
1 cup walnuts, chopped
1 tablespoon brown sugar, reserved

- Preheat oven to 350 degrees.
- Grease a standard 5 x 10 loaf pan with shortening.
- Place chopped dates in a large mixing bowl and pour hot tea over and leave to soak for 15 minutes.
- Add butter, brown sugar, vanilla and egg. Mix just until combined.
- In a separate bowl, sift flour and spices together.
- Add dry ingredients to creamed mixture, beating gently until smooth.
- Stir in nuts.
- Turn into the greased loaf pan.
- Sprinkle with the brown sugar and bake for approximately 45 minutes to 1 hour, tenting the loaf gently with foil after 30 minutes to prevent over browning.
- When a toothpick inserted in the center comes out clean, the loaf is done.
- Let loaf cool in pan for 10 minutes, then turn onto a wire rack to cool completely.
- Slice and serve with butter or Orange Cream Cheese Spread.

Orange Cream Cheese Spread

4 ounces cream cheese, softened
2 tablespoons sour cream
3 tablespoons sugar
2 teaspoons orange zest
1/2 teaspoon orange liqueur (Grand Marnier is my favorite)

- Mix all ingredients together with mixer until smooth and well combined.
- The spread may be refrigerated up to two weeks.
- Tea sandwiches can be made by slicing bread and cutting slices into halves or triangles and spreading Orange Cream Cheese Spread between layers.

Lemon Blueberry Muffins

*E*very summer when I was growing up, the family would make our way to Ethridge, Tennessee where our great friends the Bensons had a beautiful blueberry orchard.

I have an obsession with blueberry picking. Once I get started, I just cannot stop. And the same way goes when it comes to a platter of these blueberry muffins.

2 cups plus 2 tablespoons all-purpose flour
1 ½ teaspoon baking powder
1/2 teaspoon salt
3/4 cup whole milk
1 large egg
1/2 teaspoon vanilla extract
1 stick unsalted butter, room temperature
1 cup sugar
2 tablespoons lemon zest
1 ½ cups fresh blueberries, washed and patted dry

- Preheat oven to 400 degrees.
- Spray muffin pans lightly with cooking spray or use paper liners.
- Sift 2 cups flour, baking powder and salt for a dry mixture into a bowl and set aside.
- In a separate bowl blend milk, egg and vanilla for a wet mixture.
- With a mixer, cream together the butter and sugar until light and smooth.
- Add the dry mixture alternating with the wet mixture, mixing on low speed and scraping down the bowl to blend evenly. Continue to blend on medium speed for about 2 minutes until the batter is smooth.
- In a bowl scatter the 2 tablespoons flour over berries and toss to coat.
- Gently fold berries and zest into the batter.
- Scoop batter into 12 regular sized muffin cups using large stainless steep scoop.
- Bake for 18 to 20 minutes or until light golden brown.
- Let cool in pan for 5 minutes and remove.
- Drizzle with glaze.

See Lemon Glaze recipe next page

Lemon Glaze

1 tablespoon lemon juice
1/2 cup powdered sugar

Mix ingredients together with small whisk and drizzle over cooled muffins.

Tip

Zest is the outermost yellow part of the lemon.
The pith which is white is bitter. Use a zester or small
handheld grater to remove the yellow zest only.

The Roses of Liberty Hill

We lived on Liberty Hill in one of the first brick homes. My fraternal grandparents, Grandma and Papa Rose, lived across the field from us in a humble farm house. Grandma planted mint along their back porch which ran all the way across the back of the house.

Since there were no gutters, when the rain came it poured over the side of the house and the smell of fresh mint waffled through the air. Heaven! To this day the smell of mint brings back fond memories of sitting on their porch after a new rain.

Grandma Rose cooked on a wood burning stove. For the life of me, I do not know how, but some of the best food came out of that kitchen. Her Big Ol' Tea Cakes were the best thing I ever ate. Each one was the size in diameter of a large oatmeal box where they would later be fitted for fresh keeping.

She never threw anything away and was an expert recycler before her time. The apple does not fall far from the tree; I never want anything to go to waste.

An Amish family now owns the farm. I visit each summer to buy okra and other vegetables that Daddy no longer grows. The old home place was torn down to build an Amish house. A tree where Daddy peeled apples with Grandma is still there.

Sourdough Bread

This is the recipe that Mama makes for Sunday lunch, a tradition passed down from Grandmommie.

Mama received a sourdough starter years ago from a church friend — and continues to share with other families near and far. It's often gifted with a fresh loaf of bread.

This recipe has won many blue ribbons in the Giles County Fair over the years. A winning loaf of sourdough bread is achievable. It takes time, patience and practice, but it's well worth the effort.

Every first Sunday in July, Mama triples the instructions for the Johnson Family Reunion. Most of the bread is eaten with our covered-dish meal, but it also brings a high dollar in the annual auction.

And, oh yes, there's another blessing for your effort, it's aroma while rising on a Sunday morning beats any alarm clock.

See recipe next page

Johnson family reunion, July, 1971

Sourdough Bread

The original sourdough starter:

1 cup warm water
1 package yeast (2 ¼ teaspoon)
3/4 cup sugar
1 cup bread flour

• Measure all into a preferably glass bowl or jar (just for fun, so you can see what is happening).
• Cover with plastic wrap and leave for 24 hours at room temperature and up to 3 days.

To make sourdough bread:

1 cup starter
1 ½ cups warm water and 1 package yeast (2 ¼ teaspoons)
1/2 cup sugar
1/2 cup oil (vegetable or canola)
1 tablespoon salt

• Stir yeast and water together to dissolve yeast. Add sugar, oil, starter and mix well.

At this point, feed your starter (see how to do so next page) and let the starter rest for at least 6 hours.

• Sift salt into 6 cups of flour adding one cup flour at a time to liquid ingredients using a wooden spoon to incorporate until the mixture becomes a ball of dough. Brush top with oil and cover with a towel.
• Let stand at room temperature overnight or for at least 6 hours. Do not refrigerate.
• Punch down and turn out onto floured surface, knead dough 6 to 8 times.
• Using a serrated knife, divide into 3 equal parts.
• Knead each part a couple of times and shape into loaves or rolls.
• Place in pans (loaf or round) greased with shortening and brush tops with butter.

• Let rise 6 to 8 hours or until double in bulk. Do not cover and place in a draft free place to rise.

> *Due to variables in the weather, sometimes it can take up to 10 hours to rise.*

• Bake in preheated 350 degree oven for 20 to 25 minutes or until rolls are golden brown or bread sounds hollow when thumped. Tops will be hard when just out of oven.

• Serve rolls immediately while hot. Let bread cool in pan for 15 minutes then turn out on rack to cool completely.

• Coat tops with butter before completely cooled. Bread must be cooled to slice properly.

• Both bread and rolls freeze beautifully.

How to feed starter:

Store in refrigerator and remove every 3 to 7 days to feed.

> **1/2 cup sugar**
> **1 cup warm water**
> **3 tablespoons instant potatoes or 1 package of yeast.**
> **1 cup bread flour**

• Mix all ingredients well before adding to starter. Then mix into the starter.

• Let stand out of refrigerator all day (8 to 12) hours. The mixture will become bubbly.

• Use one cup for making bread and return remaining starter to refrigerator until time to feed again. If not making bread, just return starter to refrigerator after the starter has rested all day.

• You may build up as much as 4 cups of starter.

• After 4 cups, you must use the extra starter, give away or dispose of all but 1 cup and begin the feeding process again.

• You may mix more than 1 batch at a time, but in separate bowls if you have extra starter. Always keep at least 1 cup for feeding.

• Starter must be fed continually to be kept active.

Mini Cinnamon Muffins

Mini Cinnamon Muffins are a fancy replacement for cinnamon toast. These little jewels are fun to eat — just one or a whole handful. I find them the perfect extra touch for a brunch menu.

See recipe next page

Mini Cinnamon Muffins

6 tablespoons unsalted butter, melted
4 tablespoons unsalted butter, melted
1 cup sugar
1 tablespoon plus 1 teaspoon ground cinnamon
1 ½ cups all purpose flour
2 teaspoons baking powder
1/2 teaspoon salt
1/2 cup buttermilk
1 large egg

- Preheat oven to 375 degrees.
- Use cooking spray to grease a mini-muffin tin.
- In a small bowl, combine 1/2 cup sugar and 1 tablespoon cinnamon and set aside.
- In a large bowl, combine flour, baking powder, salt and remaining teaspoon cinnamon; whisk to combine.
- In a small bowl, combine 6 tablespoons butter, the remaining 1/2 cup sugar, buttermilk and egg; whisk to combine.
- Using a large rubber spatula, fold butter mixture into flour mixture, use as few strokes as possible. The mixture will be lumpy.
- Spoon 1 tablespoon batter into each prepared cup, and bake until tops are nicely golden, from 8 to 10 minutes. Instead of a tablespoon, use small stainless steel scoop to spoon batter into muffin pan evenly.
- Remove from oven and let cool in pan for 10 minutes before transferring onto a wire rack.
- Dip top of each muffin in remaining 4 tablespoons melted butter and roll in reserved cinnamon mixture.

Doe Doe's Banana Nut Bread

When Alton and I married; I got a bonus, another son — Robert Wade. Doe Doe is Robert Wade's grandmother. Here's to Robert Wade with a favorite recipe from his mother's family.

    2 cups all-purpose flour
    3 teaspoons baking powder
    3/4 cup or 1 ½ stick unsalted butter, softened
    1 cup dark brown sugar, packed
    2 eggs, beaten
    1 cup bananas, mashed and mixed with 1 teaspoon lemon
        juice (3 large bananas)
    1 cup pecans, chopped (optional)
    1 teaspoon vanilla extract

- Preheat oven to 350 degrees.
- Grease then coat with flour a 9 x 5 loaf pan.
- Cream butter and brown sugar, add bananas and then, dry ingredients.
- Add eggs and vanilla and beat until well combined.
- Stir in nuts.
- Turn into prepared pan.
- Bake for 50 minutes or until toothpick inserted in the middle comes out clean.
- Take from oven and allow to cool for ten minutes.
- Turn out on a rack to cool completely before slicing.

Tip

I prefer to use cooking spray to grease my pan.
Then sprinkle with granulated sugar for a
crispy, sweet crust.

Cream Cheese Banana Bread

I always keep a bottle of Creme De Banana on hand for Banana Pudding or Bananas Foster. Our favorite banana bread recipe also makes use of the tasty stash.

> 3/4 cup butter, softened
> 1 (8 ounce) package cream cheese, softened
> 2 cups sugar
> 2 large eggs
> 3 cups all-purpose flour
> 1/2 teaspoon baking powder
> 1/2 teaspoon baking soda
> 1/2 teaspoon salt
> 4 medium ripe bananas (blackened)
> 1 cup pecans, chopped
> 1/2 teaspoon vanilla extract
> 1 cup golden raisins
> 1 teaspoon Creme De Banana liquor

- Preheat oven to 350 degrees.
- Prepare two loaf pans with shortening and then coat with flour (or conversely use one loaf pan and four mini loaf pans).
- Mash bananas with fork.
- Beat butter and cream cheese in mixer until creamy. Gradually add sugar, beating until fluffy. Add eggs; beat until blended.
- Combine flour with baking powder, baking soda and salt.
  - Gradually add flour mixture to butter mixture, beating at low speed until well blended.
    - Stir in bananas, raisins, pecans, vanilla and liquor.
      - Spoon batter into the two prepared loaf pans.
        - Bake for 1 hour or until done. Before removing from pans, cool bread on wire rack for 10 minutes.

The Bell Tower

For two centuries, this bell rang each day to call the Harding and then the Jackson families in for meals to what is now a restored kitchen at The Belle Meade Plantation where I teach biscuit baking lessons.

Visiting school children climb the four steep stone steps to ring the bell three times, a part of our education class ritual.

The kitchen has an open window and though I don't always love the clanging of the bell, I do enjoy the children who are empowered to make the bell ring loud enough to be heard for miles.

Olive Cake

On an adventure to Burgundy, France, we found a home away from home. While traveling with a captain/sommelier/chef/hostess and deckhand, we had one of the most delicious midday meals of our life: lentil soup, a beautiful fall salad and this savory loaf.

1 ½ cups flour, sifted
1 tablespoon baking powder
1/3 cup olive oil
3/4 cup dry white wine
3/4 cup pitted olives, chopped
3/4 cup ham, finely chopped
1 cup Gruyere cheese, shredded
4 eggs, beaten

• Preheat the oven to 400 degrees.
• In a small bowl sift flour and baking powder together.
• In a mixing bowl, blend together olive oil, wine, green olives, ham and cheese.
• Add flour mixture to the liquid ingredients and mix until well blended.
• Add eggs and blend until smooth.
• Place mixture in a greased 9 x 5 loaf pan.
• Bake for 45 minutes or until toothpick inserted comes out clean.
• Turn out after 5 minutes.
• Best served hot or at room temperature.

Focaccia Bread

Focaccia is certainly not a typical Southern bread, but having traveled to Italy on several occasions, I find it to be one of the most wonderful foods in the world to devour.

The variations are endless. Focaccia can be served with fresh roasted vegetables, as a sandwich bread or as an appetizer dipped in olive oil and fresh ground pepper.

Sometimes I replace the sun-dried tomatoes with or in addition to black olives and roasted red peppers. Oh my goodness!

See recipe next page

Focaccia Bread

Bread

> 2 cups warm water
> 1 envelope dry yeast (2 ¼ teaspoons)
> 5 cups bread flour, sifted, plus as needed for dusting the
>   work space
> 2 tablespoon sugar
> 2 teaspoons kosher salt
> 2 tablespoons olive oil
> 1/2 cup sun-dried tomatoes, chopped, or 1/2 cup black olives,
>   chopped, or 1/2 cup roasted red peppers, chopped, or a
>   1/2 cup combination

Topping

> 1 tablespoon olive oil
> 1 tablespoon rosemary, coarsely chopped
> 1 teaspoon kosher salt

- To make the dough, combine the water and yeast in the bowl of a
  stand mixer.
- Stir to distribute the yeast and let the mixture sit for a few minutes to
  dissolve.
- Add the flour, sugar and salt.
- Mix on low speed with a dough hook until a smooth elastic dough is formed,
  about 10 to 15 minutes.
- Stir in the sun-dried tomatoes (or some combination — see above).
- Dust the surface of the dough with a sprinkling of flour, cover the bowl
  tightly with plastic wrap and let the dough rise at room temperature
  until it doubles in bulk, about 1 hour.
- Transfer the dough to a floured work surface sifted with flour.

Continued on next page

Focaccia Bread (con't)

- Press the dough out into a rough square about 2 inches thick. Pull each of the four corners in toward the center. Turn the dough over so the upper surface is smooth.
- Drape the ball of dough with plastic and let it rest until it has relaxed about 30 minutes.
- Brush a rimmed baking sheet liberally with 2 tablespoons of olive oil. Uncover the dough and spread. Pull the dough into a rectangle about the same dimensions as your pan. Lift the dough into the pan and stretch it out into an even layer that fills the pan.
- Brush the dough with olive oil and sprinkle rosemary evenly over oiled surface. Drap plastic wrap over the surface and let rise until it has nearly doubled in size, about 30 minutes.
- Preheat the oven to 350 degrees. Position a rack in the bottom third of the oven.
- Before placing the focaccia in the oven, use your fingertips to press dimples into the dough in a random pattern. Sprinkle the salt over the surface.
- Bake until the edges are slightly golden in color, 12 to 15 minutes. Remove from the oven and cool on a rack for about 10 minutes.
- Cut into squares and serve.

My first-born came into the world only minutes after St. Patrick's Day in 1986. It was a blustery night, but a beautiful sunshiny day on March 18. There was no better feeling than to give birth to a healthy baby boy!

As expected, he was a rambunctious little fellow. He had beautiful blue eyes and blond curly hair. He never met a stranger and could talk to a telephone pole. He was the class clown and often got into trouble for talking too much.

Britton was a Boy Scout and a member of the Giles County High School Band. He was first seat trombone and played the marching baritone. As a member of the youth at First Baptist Church, he traveled on many a mission trip in the US and abroad. On one occasion, upon returning from a mission trip, he came home with an empty suitcase. I asked where his clothes were. He said he left them for someone who needed them more.

Britton loved life, but a dark time came after his Dad and I divorced. Britton committed suicide on September 17, 2005. He was a freshman at Martin Methodist College. Today we endow a scholarship that is given in his name each year.

The world as I knew it turned upside down. I lay on the floor crying my eyes out, praying I would awake from this nightmare. But it was real. I would never see my sweet Britt Britt again on this earth.

Britton on a mission trip in Brazil

Through the grace of God and the many prayers of friends and family, I picked myself up and resumed life. I went back to work to keep myself busy. Our entire family, especially Britton's younger brother Blake, struggled to accept that Britton was not coming back home. My heart had a hole in it that would never be filled.

One realm in which I found solace — besides my faith — was baking. I started baking bread, cakes and pies and giving them away to friends and neighbors. Baking kept my mind occupied.

During this time, a bright star came into my life and that was my husband, the love of my life, Alton. He encouraged me every day to keep baking (and he didn't mind partaking in those baked goods either). We married and moved to Nashville. When I moved, I left behind my position as Regional Director of Tourism for South Central Tennessee. Uncertain of my working future, I continued a therapeutic love for baking and cooking.

My healthy distraction soon turned into a business — The Belle Meade Cake Lady. I started making specialty cakes, caramel and coconut, and a few favorite pies. My first Thanksgiving arrived with over 300 cake orders. I produced them all in my home kitchen. This was no longer therapy, it was stressful. I'm not a quitter, but it was not feasible for me to continue at that pace.

At the same time, Alton needed help at Belle Meade Plantation. Under his leadership, we opened The Belle Meade Winery and I've never looked back. I have the chance to continue my love of cooking by developing recipes with wine.

To this day I have calls for my cakes and pies, but I only bake for family and a few special friends. Baking and cooking is therapy again. Britton loved everything that I made. So today, as I bake for my culinary classes, the love that goes into it is always for Britton.

Biscuits

Big Ol' Biscuit Love Story

My family talks about some kind of fine eating when it comes to home-made biscuits. I was fated for sure. In the fourth grade, I won a blue ribbon in the Pulaski, Tennessee 4-H Club's best biscuit contest.

There were proper biscuit baking rules for the situation. Bacon grease was to be carefully smoothed across the biscuit top to insure that they were evenly browned. Paper doilies were brought in for presentation.

As far as we know, Grandmommie made this recipe family gold and eventually turned it into a science by precisely whipping out five biscuits each morning for her and my granddaddy, two for her and three for Granddaddy.

We could always find a fresh batch of biscuits or cornbread in Grandmommie's round bread keeper on her well-worn stovetop.

My Mama made a pan of biscuits everyday when my brother and I were growing up. Breakfast would be rounded out with gravy, eggs and sometimes sausage or bacon.

I did the same for my boys and now I make them on weekends, for holidays and special events. Turns out, I've been making this biscuit recipe all my life.

My Big Ol' Southern Biscuit

2 cups self-rising flour
1/4 cup shortening
2/3 to 3/4 cup whole milk

- Preheat the oven to 450 degrees.
- Measure and always remember to sift 2 cups of self-rising flour into a mixing bowl. Add in 1/4 cup of shortening (use Wonder Cup for measurement) using a pastry blender or two forks until the particles of shortening are the size of grains of rice or peas.
- At this point, one tablespoon of herbs (see Herb Biscuit recipe next page) and/or 1/2 cup cheese can be added.
- Slowly add the milk and stir with a large spoon until the flour/shortening mixture is thoroughly moistened. Do not over mix.
- Turn the dough from the bowl onto floured parchment paper or a pastry mat.
- Using as few strokes as possible with floured rolling pin, roll the dough out onto a uniform thickness of 1/2 to 3/4 inch.
- Cut the biscuits using a floured cutter (do not twist the cutter) and transfer to a shallow baking pan. Select cutter size depending on the condiment used.
- Keep re-rolling dough and cutting the biscuits until there is that piece of dough leftover. We call that the ugly biscuit, but it's our favorite. The crevices absorb the jam or jelly so we always fight over that one.
- Arrange the biscuits on the pan so that each biscuit is slightly touching the one next to it. They like to be cozy.
- Place the pan in the oven for 10 to 14 minutes or until lightly browned.
- Remove the biscuits from the oven and brush with the melted honey butter (page 150).
- Then remove biscuits to platter unless you are using a baking stone, otherwise the bottoms will harden.

Tip

To Reheat: Grandmommie never used a microwave.
She always said to first, "wet their little faces" by sprinkling water
across their tops before placing them in a preheated oven
at 350 degrees for 5 to 7 minutes.

Generational Herb Habit

*M*y first recollection of herbs was the dill that Grandmommie used to make pickles.

On the other hand, Mama grew dill, parsley, chives, oregano and basil. She did not use them for seasoning, but rather as a garnish to add greenery and aroma to a flower arrangement.

Her parsley was prolific even at Thanksgiving and Christmas and she used them as beautiful garnishes for the turkey and ham platters.

Today, I love growing rosemary, parsley, basil, chives, thyme, and oregano in my small herb garden for easy picking in our courtyard. During growing season, any individual or combination of herbs make for fresh flavors when chopped and added into the original biscuit recipe.

Rosemary in winter; parsley and chives, together in spring; and basil in summer are some of my favorite additions.

Herb Biscuits

chop and measure 3 tablespoons herbs (one or a combination)

• Add to the flour after cutting in shortening and before adding milk.

Sweet Potato Biscuits

These flavorful biscuits came into my life when my son Blake's Great Great Aunt Nell brought them to the family table on Christmas morning of 1983. Aunt Nell's specialty has become a regular bit of something extraordinary whenever we celebrate.

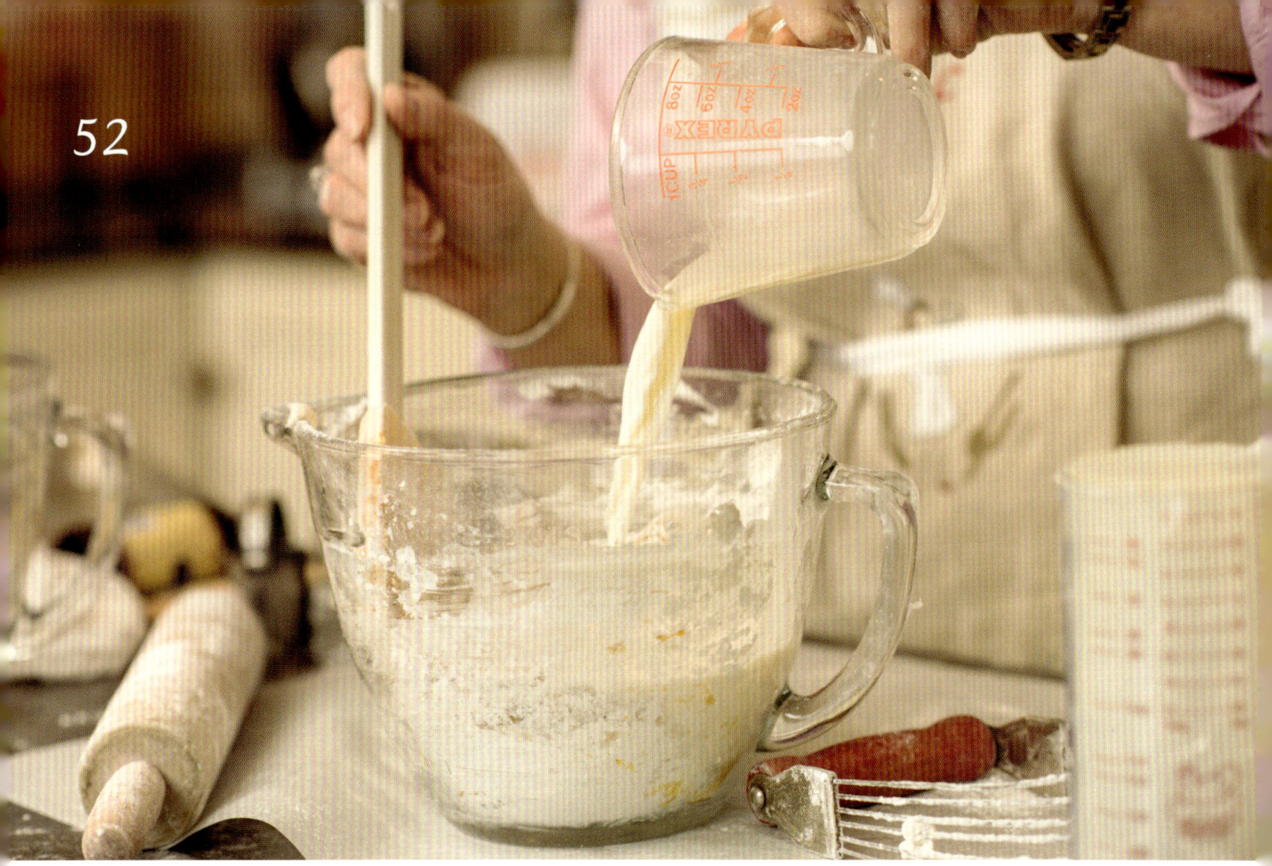

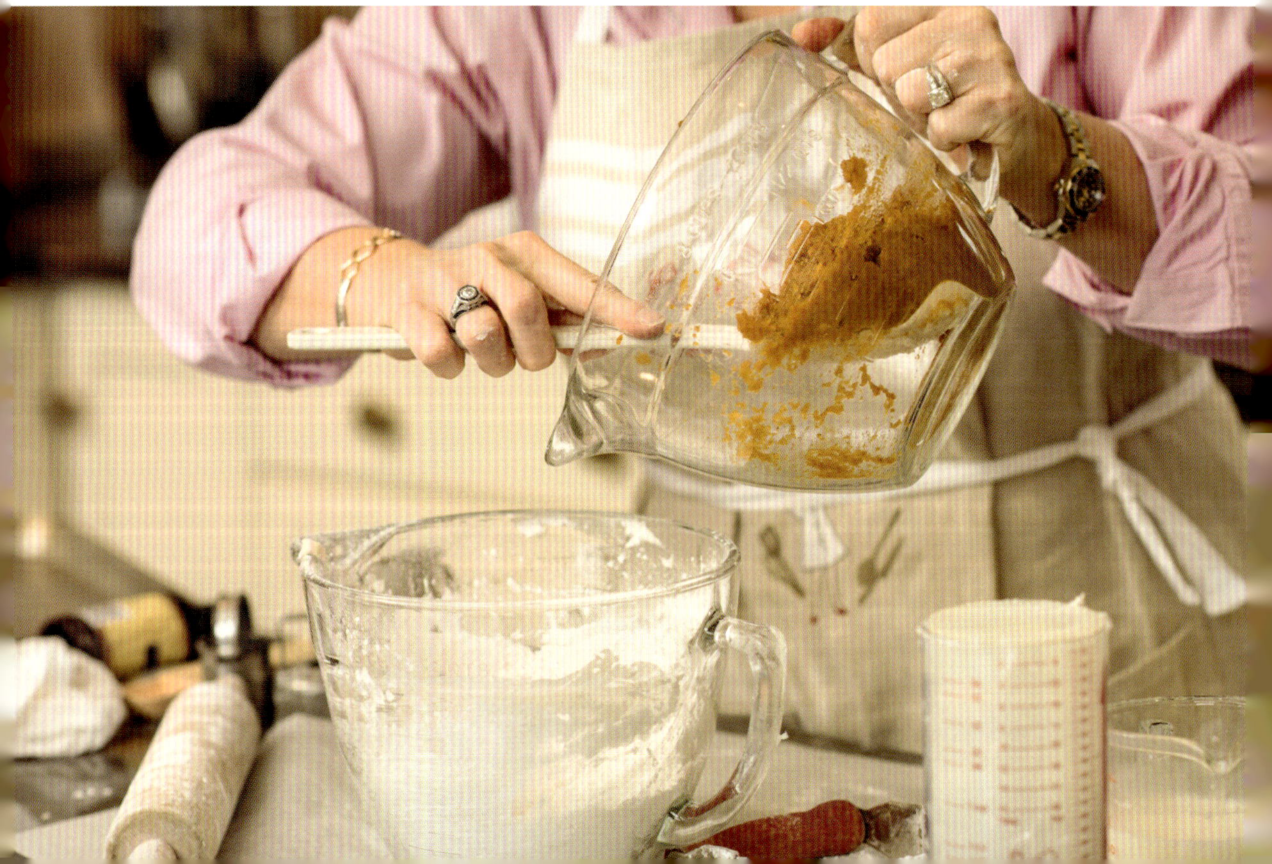

Sweet Potato Biscuits

2 cups self-rising flour, sifted
1/4 cup shortening
1 medium sweet potato measuring 1/2 cup, baked
   and mashed
1 tablespoon butter, softened
1 tablespoon sugar
1/2 teaspoon cinnamon
1/2 teaspoon vanilla extract
1/2 cup whole milk

- Preheat oven to 450 degrees. Do not grease the pan.
- Measure and sift 2 cups of self-rising flour into mixing bowl. Add 1/4 shortening and cut into the flour using a pastry blender or two forks until the mixture resembles the consistency of rice or peas.
- Peel and mash the sweet potato measuring 1/2 cup.
- In a separate bowl, add mashed sweet potato, butter, sugar, vanilla and cinnamon. Blend well.
- Add the sweet potato mixture to the flour mixture and gently stir.
- Add milk, stirring just until the mixture is moistened. Do not over mix.
- Turn the dough from the bowl onto the floured pastry mat or secured parchment paper.
- With a floured rolling pin, using as few strokes as possible, roll the dough out to a uniform thickness of 1/2 inch.
- Personal preference for biscuit cutter size is called for when cutting out biscuits. I prefer tea sized (small). When cutting, do not twist the cutter. One simple stroke of the cutter will produce the first biscuit which will begin the line up on a baking pan. These guys like to be cozy.
- Place the pan on middle rack in oven for 10 to 15 minutes or until golden brown.
- Remove from oven and place on rack to cool.
- Use pastry brush to coat biscuits with honey butter (page 150).
- Serve with country ham spread (page 138).

Heavy Cream Biscuits

Granddaddy loved to teach his grandchildren how to milk the cow he always had. He really just got a big kick out of squirting milk in our faces. Grandmommie would pour the milk into a wide-mouth glass gallon jar. She would leave it out overnight to cool, using the cream that would rise to the top for making butter, whipped cream or buttermilk for baking.

1/2 pint heavy whipping cream
2 cups self-rising flour, sifted

- Preheat oven to 450 degrees.
- Do not grease pan.
- Mix ingredients with hands until just blended. Turn out onto floured pastry board.
- Roll out in desired cutter size and cut into a little more than 1/2 inch thick biscuit.
- Bake for 10 to 12 minutes or until light golden brown.

Cream Cheese Bacon Biscuits

I relish experimenting with recipes in the kitchen. We love biscuits with bacon, so, I thought — why not bake them together?

This recipe came about by using cream cheese instead of shredded cheddar cheese and the result was a smooth tasting biscuit.

In the summer, I get a thrill out of making neighbors these biscuits as mini BLTs stacked with homegrown tomatoes and lettuce. They serve up beautifully as quick pick-ups for cocktail parties too.

2 cups self-rising flour
2 ounces cream cheese, room temperature
4 tablespoons unsalted butter, room temperature
3/4 cup buttermilk
6 slices bacon, cooked, but not super crispy and
**   coarsely chopped**

• Preheat oven to 450 degrees.
• Sift flour into large bowl.
• Cut butter and cream cheese into flour using pastry blender.
• You may use your hands or use a pastry cutter to incorporate cream cheese and butter until the mixture resembles the consistency of peas.
• Add buttermilk and mix with wooden spoon just until incorporated.
• Stir in bacon.
• Turn out dough onto a heavily floured pastry mat or secured parchment paper. Work just enough flour into dough to handle.
• Roll out into 1/2 inch thickness. Cut out with desired size biscuit cutter using all the dough.
• Do not twist cutter while cutting.
• Place on un-greased cookie sheet next to each other.
• Bake 14 to 16 minutes or until golden brown.

Sour Cream 7 UP Biscuits

I am devoted to my good ol' fashion southern biscuit recipe, but on occasion it is fun to think outside the box. This is a quick recipe that produces a light and fluffy biscuit. It is a great vehicle for country ham, sausage, bacon, scrambled eggs or even a drizzle of honey.

The citrus flavor from the 7 UP also pairs well with blackberry or blueberry jelly or jam. And when tomatoes are in season, there is nothing like the freshness of a juicy tomato on this biscuit.

Sour Cream 7 UP Biscuits

4 cups Bisquick
1 cup sour cream
6 ounces 7UP

- Preheat oven to 425 degrees.
- Using a pastry blender or two forks, mix the sour cream into the biscuit mix until the mixture is crumbly.
- Add 7UP all at once. Stir quickly with a large wooden spoon.
- Turn out onto lightly floured board and quickly knead 6 to 10 times. Work enough flour into mix so as to handle the dough easily without being too sticky. Do not over mix or biscuits will be tough.
- Pat into large rectangle about 1/2 inch thick and cut into 20 equal square pieces using knife coated in flour. Alternately, the rectangle can be cut into fewer and larger biscuit squares or more and smaller biscuit squares. The dough may also be cut using a round biscuit cutter.
- Place biscuits on an un-greased baking sheet leaving a little space between each biscuit.
- Bake 8 to 10 minutes or adjust according to size until light golden.
- Biscuits can remain on the hot pan until ready to eat, or placed in a basket and covered until ready to eat. Later their little faces can also be sprinkled with water for reheating in the oven.

Cheesy Pimento Biscuits

Pimento Cheese is a favorite Southern staple for me. The versions are endless. Grandmommie and Mama's recipe included three ingredients - Velveeta Cheese, grated on a box grater, mayo and chopped pimento peppers, spread between two slices of crustless white bread and cut in half.

Presented this way, our family pimento recipe starred in many an afternoon tea, cover dish meal or quick bite for lunch. From a mile away, I could spot that flat Tupperware container with those mouth watering sandwiches tucked inside.

I have found that this biscuit is the perfect pimento cheese vehicle for a dollop of pepper jelly. Savory and spicy-sweet, this version makes for an all time best appetizer.

Cheesy Pimento Biscuits

2 ¼ cups self-rising flour, sifted
1/8 teaspoon garlic powder
1/8 teaspoon onion powder
1 cup sharp cheddar cheese, shredded
1/2 cup unsalted butter, chilled
1 cup buttermilk
1 (2 ounce) jar of diced pimentos, undrained

- Preheat oven to 450 degrees.
- Sift flour, garlic powder, onion salt together into a large bowl.
- Add cheese and stir to coat cheese with flour.
- Cut butter into small pieces and add to flour mixture.
- Using a pastry blender, cut butter into mixture until crumbly.
- Cover and chill for 10 minutes.
- Stir together buttermilk and undrained pimentos.
- Add liquid to dry ingredients, stirring until moistened.
- Turn dough onto a lightly floured surface and knead 3 to 4 times, adding more flour as needed.
- Pat dough into a 3/4 inch thick rectangle.
- Sprinkle lightly with flour, then fold dough over onto itself, kneading and patting into a 3/4 thick rectangle again.
- On a lightly floured surface, roll dough into 1/2 inch thick rectangle.
- Cut with the desired size round biscuit cutter.
- Place on parchment lined baking sheet, allowing a small space between biscuits so that they can expand and rise.
- Bake for 12 to 14 minutes or until lightly browned.

Tip

I find it handy to have a variety of biscuit cutter sizes,
but the tea size (1 ½ inch) is my favorite and
essential for Southern kitchens everywhere.

Cheddar Garlic Biscuits

When I was a teenager and then a young married, my family traveled from Pulaski to Huntsville to be entertained and to go out for a meal. The trip was 45 minutes on a two-lane road and we thought about the garlic rolls at Red Lobster along the way.

Red Lobster was a big deal since we did not have seafood available to us in our small town. I was determined to make those at home. So *voilá*.

2 cups self-rising flour, sifted
1/4 cup shortening
3/4 cup whole milk or buttermilk
1 cup cheddar cheese, grated
1/4 cup butter, softened
1/2 teaspoon garlic powder

- Preheat oven to 425 degrees.
- Spray baking sheet lightly with non-stick cooking spray.
- In a large bowl, add flour and cut in the shortening with a pastry blender or two forks until flour resembles rice or peas.
- Stir in cheese and milk until moistened and the dough holds together.
- Drop by heaping tablespoons onto the baking sheet.
- Bake for 10 to 12 minutes or until tops are golden brown.
- Remove from oven and brush with garlic butter

Garlic Butter — mix butter and garlic powder until well blended.

Appetizers

Sausage Pinwheels

My introduction to Sausage Pinwheels is ever twined to Christmas morning. My son Blake's Nana Taylor presented them at our annual family gathering, but she used a buttermilk biscuit recipe.

Using My Big Ol' Southern Biscuit recipe, I began to make them for my boys on weekends and for the occasional appetizer. Every year late in November, when it is hog killing time, I pick up sausages from a family in North Giles County and freeze for later. A fresh sausage vendor will provide the best result for preparing these pinwheels.

These days, I never wait for a special occasion. At Harpeth Presbyterian in Nashville, we often sign up to contribute for an early church breakfast and because Alton loves them, I make sure that I have those pinwheels ready to go. Even so, they do freeze well!

See recipe next page

Sausage Pinwheels

1 My Big Ol' Southern Biscuit Recipe (Page 43)
1 pound of ground sausage

• Preheat oven to 375 degrees.
• Prepare biscuit recipe to the place where the dough is to be rolled out.
  Roll dough out on a heavily floured surface into a rectangle with about
  1/8 inch thickness.
• Sprinkle uncooked sausage over dough leaving a 1/2 inch border free.
• Roll up the long side and pinch seams together.
• Slice 1/4 to 1/2 inch thick rounds. Use a serrated knife to slide right through.
  If a serrated is not available, a plain but sharp knife will provide slices that
  must be reshaped into flat circles by hand.
• Bake on un-greased baking sheet for 25 minutes or until lightly browned.

Smaller Pinwheels

Half with sausage and half with sausage and cheese: cut the rectangle of
dough in half lengthwise and sprinkle the sausage on both halves — scatter
1 cup of cheddar cheese over the sausage of one of the halves — roll and
slice into 1/4 to 1/2 inch slices — when using cheese, first spray baking sheet
with cooking spray.

Tip

When reheating, Grandmommie always told me to "wet their little faces"
and place back into the oven to reheat. "And they will taste like
they did when you first made them," she said.
If freezing, be sure to defrost halfway before reheating.

Salmon Croissant

This appetizer was part of an exceptional experience on a six passenger barge hotel a la Marne River in the Champagne Region of France. Every afternoon our chef would bring us together for "bubbles du jour and canapes".

As usual, I popped into the kitchen for any recipe that could be shared. The canapé remains in my heart.

> **sheet of puff pastry**
> **smoked salmon (preferably Scottish as this variety holds**
> **the flavor when heated)**
> **small jar of horseradish cream**
> **1 large spring of dill**
> **1 egg**

- Preheat oven to 400 degrees.
- Roll out puff pastry onto parchment paper into a thin, rectangular shape about an 1/8 inch thick.
- Cut small triangles. The base of the triangle will determine the size, no more than two inches long.
- Lay all the triangles with bases facing down and brush with horseradish cream.
- Lay a small slice of salmon onto the triangle. The slice should be smaller than the pastry.
- Gently roll the bottom toward the top to get that familiar croissant shape.
- Place on baking tray with non-stick parchment and brush with egg wash.*
- Bake for 25 minutes or until golden brown.
- Remove from the oven and leave to cool for five minutes; then place in a basket and sprinkle with chopped dill. Some may pop open as they bake. They are still delicious!
- Alway serve with a crisp, well-chilled champagne. Any sparkling wine will do as long as it is a dry one.

Tip

*To make an egg wash, break egg into a small bowl and add 1 tablespoon water or milk and whisk briskly to mix well.

Aunt Nedra's Cheese Crisps

*M*y mother's sister Aunt Nedra was a red-headed firecracker and keeper of family traditions. As assistant to the President of Martin Methodist College for 30 years, she entertained countless visiting dignitaries and students.

She was well traveled and an expert in hospitality. Family members tell me that I am more like her than anyone in the family. Alton says that I was mixed up at birth - "must have been Nedra's."

See recipe next page

Aunt Nedra's Cheese Crisps

3 cups sharp cheddar cheese, grated
2 sticks of unsalted butter, softened
2 cups all purpose flour, sifted
1/2 teaspoon salt
1/4 teaspoon red pepper
2 cups of Rice Krispie cereal
pecan halves

• Preheat oven to 350 degrees.
• Mix all ingredients together to form one inch balls.
• Place on cookie sheet one inch apart and press with tines of a fork to make a crossed fork indention. Place a pecan half on the indention.
• Bake about 14 minutes. Remove from pan to wire rack for cooling.

Mama Cheryl Rose, Aunt Linda Yokley,
Aunt Nedra Trebing and Grandmommie

John Rochford's Fish Camp Bobbers

*J*ohn Rochford and his wife Carol are travel buddies of ours. We have shared a lot of meals and I can tell you that he loves olives. This particular crusty olive appetizer is a favorite of his and now ours too.

1 cup sharp cheddar cheese, shredded
1/2 cup flour
1/8 teaspoon or more cayenne pepper
3 tablespoons butter, softened
24 to 36 Manzanilla (small) pimiento stuffed olives

• Preheat oven to 400 degrees.
• Line cookie sheet with parchment paper.
• Add shredded cheese, flour and cayenne pepper into a food processor.
• Pulse until fine.
• Add 3 tablespoons butter and pulse to combine.
• Place olives in a strainer to remove excess juice, but do not dry.
• Place one teaspoon of cheese/flour mixture in palm of hand and flatten.
• Add olive in the middle and wrap completely.
• Roll with hands and place on cookie sheet.
• Bake for 12 to 15 minutes or until golden brown.
• Serve warm.

Tip

If not baking that day, you can place them in a freezer bag and thaw 15 minutes while preheating the oven.

Mrs. Lewis' Cheese Logs

Mrs. Alene Lewis was a spitfire. Though short in stature, she was a strong and well-respected community member. Her daughter, Lea, my childhood friend, later told me that while everyone else was outside playing; they would look inside to find Mrs. Lewis and me chatting in the kitchen. I was collecting her recipes.

Mrs. Lewis made these cheese logs for the Methodist Youth Fellowship at First United Methodist Church in Pulaski, Tennessee. She would make a double or triple recipe to fill a large paper double-bagged grocery bag for transport.

1 pound New York sharp cheddar cheese, grated
1 pound butter, softened
4 to 5 cups all purpose flour
1 egg
1 teaspoon water

- Preheat oven to 325 degrees.
- Combine cheese, butter and flour.
- Mash with fingers until all combined; adding 1 cup of flour at a time.
- Knead on floured board.
- Divide into 4 portions and roll into snakes the size of dimes.
- Slice into 1 inch logs.
- Mix egg and water together to make egg wash. Brush the egg wash on cheese logs with pastry brush.
- Bake for 20 to 25 minutes.

Bodenham Mill: Granddaddy and Alton

The old Bodenham Mill in Giles County still stands, but the waterwheel is silent. Located near my grandparents' place, The Johnson Farm, the mill was the heart of the community back in the day. The sounds of mules pulling buckboard wagons filled with wheat or corn still echo from an everyday occurrence once provided.

Not only was corn and wheat being made into corn meal and flour, but time spent at the mill waiting on the "grinding" was a rare chance for leisure time, the latest news and maybe a game of checkers.

Our village mill was driven by water that pushed a giant water wheel to go round and round, which in turn moved a carved "millstone," the catalyst for turning crops grown into cash or valuable commodities for everyday use.

Time spent at the mill waiting on the "grinding" was a rare chance for leisure. Now, the waterwheel is silent.

One of the last outings that my Grandfather requested was for my husband Alton and me to take him back to the mill. At the spry age of 95, he hoisted himself up on the loading ramp as the current owner invited him to take his time reliving the past.

Just like flour gushing from the grindstone, story after story poured from my grandfather to his granddaughter. For me, what a memory to cherish and a highlight of Alton's time with Granddaddy.

Cast Iron Skillet Cornbread

Mama's cornbread recipe was one of the first things that I learned to make when I was big enough to get up to the counter in a chair.

Sometimes I would help my Daddy Rudolph Rose get a quick supper going of cornbread and fried potatoes, if we got home before Mama.

It is best loved by us served with white or pinto beans or fried chicken.

1 large egg
1 ⅓ cup whole milk
1/4 cup plus 2 tablespoons cooking oil
1 tablespoon sugar
1 ½ cups self-rising white corn meal
1/2 cup of self rising flour

- Preheat the oven to 450 degrees.
- Put 2 tablespoons of oil in an 8 or 9 inch skillet or any pan of equal size and place into the oven for 7 to 8 minutes.
- Meanwhile, beat egg in medium bowl. Stir in milk, oil, sugar, flour and cornmeal until completely mixed. If too thick, add 1 to 2 tablespoons of milk.
- Remove hot skillet from oven and sift about 2 tablespoons of flour across the pan into the hot grease. Immediately pour batter into the pan.
- Bake 20 to 25 minutes or until golden brown. Turn out onto platter and serve with lots of butter.

Tip

For muffins or cornsticks, make as above and fill muffin
tin pan or cast iron cornstick pan 2/3 full and bake
15 to 20 minutes or until golden brown.

Left: Corn Light Bread; Right, Cast Iron Skillet Cornbread

Hot Water Cornbread

*D*addy was the youngest boy of seven children. He worked closely with Papa Rose in the garden and the fields.

After they gathered and shucked hickory cane corn in the field, Papa would hoist Daddy onto a mule, since he was not yet big enough to get there by himself, and send him on to Mr. Robert Buckner's mill at the top of Liberty Hill near Campbellsville.

Mr. Buckner would grind the corn into meal and use a small tin cup to remove his portion in lieu of payment for service. Then he would place Daddy back on the mule for the return trip to Grandma Rose so she could take that meal and make her famous hot water cornbread.

Grandma Rose served hers with beans. Later Daddy would serve his with a pork roast and greens.

2 cups white self-rising cornmeal
2 cups water
1/2 cup cooking oil

- Measure cornmeal into medium bowl.
- Boil the water and then pour the boiling water onto the cornmeal.
- Stir until soft mixture forms. If the mixture is too thick add more water.
- Test skillet or griddle by scattering some flour, if it sizzles then the pan is ready.
- Drop by large heaping tablespoon or medium stainless steel scoop onto greased skillet or griddle.
- Cook the batter like pancakes and do not press down on the cornbread.
- Cook about 3 minutes on one side and 2 minutes on the other or until golden brown.

Corn Light Bread

As the boys grew up, most Saturday mornings were spent at the base-ball and soccer fields, but by the afternoon, we headed to Franklin, Tennessee to shop, or go see a movie and eat a good old fashion barbecue plate of country ribs, slaw, baked beans and corn light bread.

Corn light bread is a specialty corn bread baked in a loaf pan. After I had my first bite, I had to pour over old recipe books so I could begin making my own.

Make no mistake, this bread is not low calorie just because it is referred to as 'light'. It has a sweet flavor more like cake. Use it to sop up the barbecue sauce served with ribs, brisket or pulled pork.

1 egg, beaten
2 cups self-rising cornmeal
1/2 cup all purpose flour
1 cup sugar
1 teaspoon salt
1/2 teaspoon baking soda
2 cups buttermilk
2 tablespoons cooking oil

- Preheat oven to 350 degrees.
- Mix all ingredients and pour into hot greased loaf pan.
- Bake for 1 hour or until brown; the top of the loaf will be flat.
- Occasionally I also bake for 40 to 45 minutes in 4 small stoneware loaf pans.
- Wait 10 minutes and turn out on wire rack.

Mexican Cornbread

$\mathcal{T}$his recipe came to me from a dear friend around 1985. Debbie Davis Graham grew up in a family of good cooks. She wrote this recipe down for me on an order form from Shields Flowers, my family's business. It's been a favorite order from my kitchen ever since.

I learned to add a secret ingredient of freshness to the recipe. Around the end of summer, before the last frost or when there are plenty of peppers still on the vine, I pick all the bell, banana and hot peppers from my Mama and Daddy's garden.

They must be washed and dried on top of paper towels. At this point, it is a smart thing to use gloves if you have any hot peppers in the bunch. Remove the seeds and membranes from the peppers and chop them finely in the food processor (be careful not to overdo) or by hand with a knife. Grandmommie used a small hand nut grinder, but would employ a hand meat grinder for large amounts.

I like to spoon those peppers into ice cube trays and freeze. After they are frozen cubes, I drop them all into a gallon freezer bag and keep frozen until some flavor is needed.

The cubes can transform a roast, soups or most importantly show up as a substitute for the canned green chiles below. Big ol' time in the winter when I serve this cornbread with beef stew or red beans and rice.

See recipe next page

Mexican Cornbread

3 cups self-rising cornmeal
1/2 teaspoon salt
1/2 teaspoon baking powder
2 tablespoons sugar
2 cups whole milk
3 eggs, beaten
1/2 cup canola oil
1 (14.75 ounce) can cream corn
1 ½ cup grated cheddar cheese
1/2 cup chopped onion
1 small drained 4 ounce can of chopped chili peppers
   or one frozen cube (see previous page)

- Preheat oven to 350 degrees. In a 2 quart bowl combine cornmeal, salt, baking powder and sugar; stir well. Add the ingredients in order as listed above and stir well after each ingredient.
- Bake in a 9 x 13 pan for 40 to 45 minutes or until golden brown.
- Remove from the oven and cool before slicing. Take time to slather on some real butter.

Grandma Rose's Hoe Cakes

For many years we filled our flour needs by doing business with the Pulaski Pearl Mill. My first memory is of 5 pound muslin bags of flour and then later, paper bags took the day. Grandma and Grandmommie used the muslin sacks for making the girls' dresses, boys' shirts, dish cloths and even diapers. One did not throw anything away that could be repurposed.

In the fall, our family loved a nighttime supper of fried potatoes, greens, pork roast and these hoe cakes. On a busy day, a favorite meal of mine includes hoe cakes and roast beef, potatoes, carrots a la crockpot.

See recipe next page

Grandma Rose's Hoe Cakes

1 ½ cups self rising cornmeal mix
1 beaten egg
1 cup buttermilk
1 tablespoon cooking oil

• Mix all ingredients together.
• Heat a greased ten inch skillet or a griddle. To tell if the pan is hot enough, sprinkle flour on the surface of the skillet or griddle and look for a sizzle.
• Spoon 1 tablespoon of the batter into small circles until the skillet or griddle is filled. Cook until tiny bubbles appear on the surface (about 2 minutes) and flip to cook the other side.

Hoe cakes can be reheated by sprinkling water on their little faces and heated at 350 for 2 minutes.

Aunt Chennie's Hushpuppies

1 ½ cups self-rising corn meal
1/2 cup self-rising flour, sifted
1/4 teaspoon salt
1/4 teaspoon pepper
1 egg, beaten
1 cup buttermilk or 3/4 cup milk
1/4 cup onion, finely chopped
1/4 cup bell pepper, finely chopped
2 tablespoons canned jalapeno or mixed peppers from garden,
    frozen in ice tray (page 84), finely chopped

- Mix all ingredients in the order listed.
- Drop by large tablespoon or medium stainless steel scoop into hot, boiling oil around 320 degrees.
- Cook about 5 minutes until the hushpuppy floats to the top of the oil and turns golden brown. Turn to cook all sides evenly.
- Serve on platter with paper towels to absorb the grease.

Zesty Cocktail Sauce

Why use plain ol' ketchup? This cocktail sauce will kick anything up a notch particularly Hushpuppies (page 92). There is nothing more appetizing…a speedy treat from the fryer, then a dab of cocktail sauce and into your mouth!

1 cup ketchup
2 tablespoons prepared horseradish
1 teaspoon Worcestershire Sauce
1 tablespoon lemon juice
1/2 teaspoon hot sauce

- Mix all ingredients well by hand. Chill and enjoy.

Photo and story next page

Aunt Chennie's Hushpuppies

*T*here is nothing like a big ol' fish fry in the summertime! Hushpuppies are mandatory.

During my childhood, my cousins and I always took advantage of a fishing hole. Our family loved to fish, whether it be the Tennessee River or Weakley Creek.

We had many a fish fry and once the fish were caught; we each had our task. Mama (Aunt Chennie) made the hushpuppies because her way was the best.

I have this recipe in my head from watching her many times over the years. They are pretty darn good.

See recipe previous page

Grandmommie and Granddaddy

My maternal Great Grandmother Florence Boatright Johnson, or Ma Johnson as she was known, could cook up whatever was handy, and my Grandfather said there was always plenty to eat.

She cooked possum, groundhog, rabbit, squirrel and even muskrat. Muskrats were lean and clean from living in the creek and eating grass. Her husband Newt Johnson, my Great Grandfather (Pa Johnson), grew a big garden every year so food was plentiful there in their Giles County, Tennessee home.

Their son, my Grandaddy, married Grandmommie when she was sixteen years of age. She had skills even then coming from a time when she had taken over care of the family when her own mother died at a young age. Her mother-in-law Ma Johnson and Grandaddy's sisters helped her out with what she had yet to learn.

Grandmommie loved to tell the early-married story of waking one morning and knowing that besides the staples (milk, sugar, flour and eggs), she was without food to prepare a meal. But before she could turn around, many meals would be provided.

A milk order from Granddaddy's delivery route, February 1, 1952.

As driver of the milk truck, Grandaddy soon stopped in to leave corn, beans, potatoes and other freshly picked vegetables from Mr. Abernathy, a neighbor up the hollow, who Grandaddy had received milk from that very morning.

In those days, they made use of a spring house, a small one room structure built over a spring. I cannot imagine how many treks Grandmommie made to the spring each day to fetch their milk and butter. She and my Granddaddy were frugal and hard workers from day one, a trait that carried over into their own family of five children, my mother being the youngest daughter.

While my mother was growing up, Grandmommie worked at the Lee Mar Shirt Factory and tended to everyone's needs, cooked, cleaned and sewed for the girls and eventually even the granddaughters.

When I was growing up there was never a question as to where my family would be on Sundays. We attended Choates Creek United Methodist Church and then would go directly up the road for dinner at Grandmommies's and Granddaddy's house.

The Sunday spread was always roast beef, potatoes and carrots, fried chicken, gravy, cream corn or corn on the cob, fried okra, butter beans or peas, homemade rolls, desserts, sweet tea and lemonade. All made by Grandmommie.

She did what she could to get ready on Saturday and then rose early on Sunday to get everything together before leaving for church.

And I was right there with Grandmommie on those Saturday mornings while my Mama and Daddy worked. Her kitchen was spotless. She taught me knife skills and how to can and

Granddaddy's milk truck, a converted car (circa 1941)

freeze the harvest from the garden. While there at their house, duty required a dusting chore which I dislike to this day. We were taught to work first and play later.

When finished with our chores, Grandaddy would take us to Fleeman's Store up the road to buy a treat, penny candy. I have dear memories of spending the night there and watching *The Lawrence Welk Show* with them as we grabbed a bowl and shelled some peas or beans.

"Idle time is the devil's workshop," Grandmommie would say.

Rolls

Grandmommie's Sunday Dinner Rolls

Grandmommie made these rolls each and every Sunday.

They were in their final rise while we were all in church. She donned an apron over her Sunday clothes and popped them in the oven when we returned to the house for dinner. In my opinion, there is no substitute for homemade rolls.

Grandmommie did not allow anything to happen on the Sabbath.

Even though we did wash the dishes, our Sundays were spent as sacred time enjoying the company of family and friends.

> **1 cup shortening**
> **1 cup sugar**
> **1 cup boiling water**
> **2 eggs, beaten**
> **2 teaspoons salt**
> **2 packages dry yeast**
> **1 cup warm water**
> **6 cups bread flour, sifted**

- In a large mixing bowl, pour boiling water over shortening, sugar and salt.
- Blend mixture and cool.
- Add beaten eggs.
- Sprinkle yeast into warm water, stir until dissolved, and add to mixture.
- Add flour and blend well.
- Cover and place in refrigerator for at least 4 hours or overnight.
- Dough will rise slightly while in the refrigerator and will keep a week to 10 days. It may be used as needed.
- These rolls need extra time to rise outside the refrigerator. About 3 hours before using, remove from the refrigerator.
- Scatter enough extra flour to make dough easy to roll out.
- Roll out into a 1/2 inch thickness.

Continued on next page

Grandmommie's Sunday Dinner Rolls (con't)

- Prepare rolls by using a round biscuit cutter. Place each roll on a baking pan, greased with shortening. Brush with melted butter or olive oil (do not cover). The rolls should not touch, but after they rise they will touch each other.
- Allow another 2 to 3 hours for rolls to rise in the pan or until they double in size.
- Bake in oven at 425 degrees for 12 to 15 minutes until light golden brown.

Impromptu Rolls

An impromptu dinner party with the neighbors calls for a quick bread to round out plates of grilled chicken, vegetables and a salad. These ingredients are staples in my kitchen and the batter, ladled into muffin tins, bakes into a fluffy roll with a bit of crunch; the perfect bread partner for any meal of the day.

> 2 cups self-rising flour, sifted
> 1/4 cup mayonnaise
> 1 cup milk
> 1 tablespoon sugar

- Preheat oven to 450 degrees.
- Mix all ingredients by hand in a mixing bowl for about 2 minutes.
- Fill muffin tins until 2/3 full and bake for 10 to 12 minutes or until golden brown.

Mama's Spoon Rolls

Mama's Spoon Rolls

My mother and her sister Nedra could get the job done. They were multi-taskers before the phrase was coined. Nedra was a silent partner for Mama's beauty shop, Curl Harbor.

They both benefitted as the shop became a hot bed of recipe commerce. This classic recipe outlives their business, a mainstay of Pulaski in the Green Acres Shopping Center for ten years.

My family lived close to Curl Harbor and I often rode my bicycle to enjoy a visit with Mama's patrons. While chatting with the ladies, I picked up quite a few recipes like this one.

My family has loved the ease of preparation and the versatility of these beautiful rolls. A hint of sugar creates the perfect sweetness in every bite and while baking, the smell will make your mouth water too.

2 cups lukewarm water
1 ½ sticks salted butter, melted
1 well beaten egg
1 (1/4 ounce) package yeast
1/4 cup sugar
4 cups self-rising flour

- Preheat the oven to 400 degrees.
- In a large bowl, dissolve yeast in the water.
- Add butter, egg and sugar and mix well. Stir in flour.
- Refrigerate for at least 2 hours or overnight.
- Stir batter before spooning into well greased muffin tins (2/3 full) and bake for 10 minutes or until golden brown.
- Serve warm.

Mary Palmer's Pop - Overs

Strong women run in both Alton's family and mine. His grandmother, Mary Palmer Sperry was adored by him and his siblings. She lost her hearing from a childhood disease, but that never slowed her down.

She is remembered, even today, by friends and family as a woman of grace and dignity who always had a sense of style. From women's suffrage to volunteering aid for returning World War II veterans, to being the grande dame to a pack of wild grandchildren; she embraced it all.

Popovers are not something that my family baked. Truth be known, I had never tried one until I baked Mary Palmer's hand written recipe. They are a tradition that came from Alton's Irish roots and are called Yorkshire Pudding in the old country. Today they are a Sunday staple at family dinners.

Though I never knew Mary Palmer, I offer this recipe as a tribute to Alton who has always been my biggest cheerleader.

Recipe on next page

Mary Palmer's Pop - Overs

3 eggs
1 cup milk
2 teaspoons salted butter, melted
1 cup flour

- Preheat oven to 425 degrees.
- Beat eggs, milk, flour and butter lightly with a whisk.
- Spray popover tin with cooking spray.
- Bake for 45 minutes.

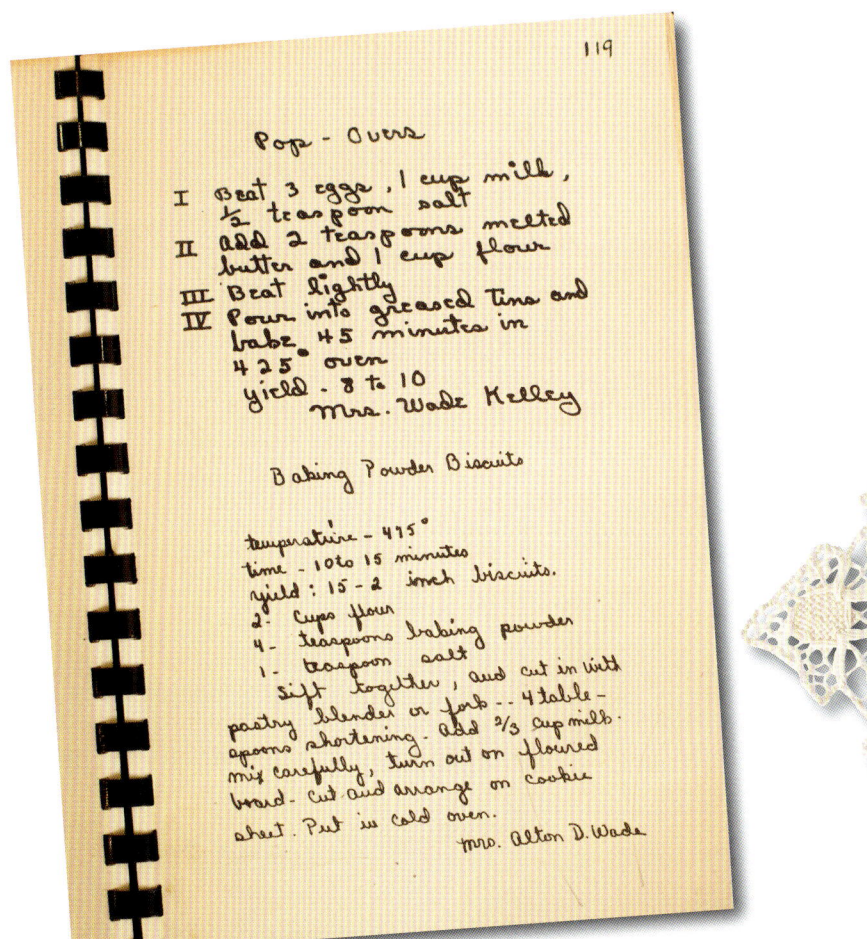

Cinnamon Rolls

Cinnamon Rolls

Prepare a recipe of Grandmommie's Sunday Dinner Rolls (page 98)

Filling for Cinnamon Rolls

1/2 cup unsalted butter, softened
1/2 cup brown sugar, packed
1/2 cup sugar
2 teaspoons cinnamon
1 cup nuts pecans, chopped
1 cup golden raisins

• Roll dough into large rectangle about 1/4 inch thick.
• Brush butter over rectangle.
• Mix sugars, cinnamon, nuts and raisins together and sprinkle over buttered rectangle.
• Roll up tightly from the long side in a jelly roll style.
• Using a serrated knife, slice into 1 inch thick slices and place into a 9 x 13 pan greased with shortening. Place rolls close together.
• Allow to rise in a warm place until the rolls are doubled in size, about 2 to 3 hours.
• Preheat oven to 425 degrees.
• Bake for 12 to 15 minutes or until light golden brown.
• From refrigerator, divide dough into halves, 1/2 for dinner rolls and 1/2 for cinnamon rolls or conversely all dinner rolls or all cinnamon rolls. If you only choose to make 1/2 of the dough into dinner rolls or cinnamon rolls, place the dough back into the refrigerator for later preparation.

Specialties

Old Fashion Fried Pies

Old Fashion Fried Pies

*N*ext door and within sight of Grandmommie and Granddaddy's house was a large peach orchard. After the peaches were picked and sold, the overripe ones were for the taking.

Grandaddy would fetch those beautiful leftovers so that Grandmommie could make her incomparable peach pie filling.

For ease these days, I use the canned fillings either cherry, apple or still my favorite, peach.

My Big Ol' Southern Biscuit recipe (page 48)
21 ounce can pie filling, fruit of your choice
1/2 teaspoon cinnamon to combine with apple and
**   peach pie filling**

• Prepare the biscuit recipe (page 48).
• Roll out the dough recipe 3/4 inches thick and cut out biscuits with a 2 ¼ inch biscuit cutter.
• Roll each cut biscuit into a thin round disk 1/8 inch thick, the size of a small saucer. Place a small saucer (approximately 5 inches) over the rolled out disk and cut around the saucer with a sharp knife to make uniform round pieces of dough.
• Place 1 tablespoon of pie filling in the center of the dough.
• Fold over in a half moon shape and seal with the tines of a fork.
• Fill large iron skillet or electric skillet with 1/2 inch canola oil and turn to medium high on iron skillet and 300 degrees on the electric skillet.
• Place about 6 fried pies into the skillet at a time. Cook on both sides until equally golden brown.
• Remove from pan onto paper towel lined platter to absorb the oil.

Pizza Dough and Breadsticks for the Boys

I used the Chef Boyardee Pizza Kit the first time I ever made pizza at home. The box contained the crust mix, sauce, pepperoni and grated Parmesan cheese. Easy to assemble, it was a favorite Friday night treat growing up. This was before Pizza Hut came to town.

A friend gave me this recipe to make my own pizza crust some 20 years ago. I happily made it countless times for my boys and their friends.

5 cups all purpose or bread flour, sifted
2 tablespoons yeast
1 tablespoon salt
2 teaspoons sugar
1/2 cup oil
1 ½ cup warm water

Pizza
- Preheat oven to 450 degrées.
- Mix together flour, yeast, salt, and sugar.
- Add the oil and warm water.
- Knead until the dough holds shape.
- Coat dough with 2 to 3 tablespoons oil and place in bowl covered with towel to rise for 20 minutes.
- Divide in half.
- Roll each pizza out onto 15 inch pizza pans or round stones. Prick with fork.
- Par bake for 4 minutes in 450 degree oven.
- Remove from oven, drizzle or brush with 1 tablespoon of olive oil. Sprinkle with Italian seasoning. Add pizza sauce, various toppings and finally cheese.

Bread Sticks
- Preheat oven to 450 degrees.
- Alternately you can use 1/2 dough for 1 pizza and 1/2 dough for breadsticks.
- Roll dough into a rectangle onto baking sheet.
- Brush with butter. Sprinkle with garlic salt, Italian seasoning and fresh parmesan cheese.
- Cut dough into 1/2 inch wide strips with a pizza cutter before you bake.
- Bake for 15 minutes.

Blackberry Cobbler

During the 1990's, I worked as the assistant to the president of Community Bank in Pulaski. At that time, the bank was expanding and they decided to sell an adjacent historical home to any Giles County resident who owned land and could bring a plan to move it. The price - one dollar.

Mama and Daddy walked into the house, fell in love with it and were awarded ownership. Then began the rigorous work to place it on a perfect site; their property of 65 acres outside of town in an old phosphate mining area was perfect.

The five mile trek was not easy. After many months and thousands of dollars, moving day arrived. The house was cut in half to move to what is now referred to as Country Club Farm.

A party-like atmosphere hovered over Pulaski. Moving day was a town spectacle and with electrical lines down as the two halves passed through town, folks yelled and waved along the route.

The home was placed back together and to this day, only one seam is visible in the front hall.

Mama and Daddy are in "hog heaven" with the house in the country. Daddy is thrilled to have a big ol' garden and the animals of his choice.

Unlike Great Uncle Willie's farm, he planted a beautifully controlled blackberry patch without a thorn in site. The berries are the size of the end of my thumb. They are easy to pick and you can fill a bucket in a flash.

Recipe on next page

Blackberry Cobbler

4 cups fresh blackberries
1 tablespoon lemon juice
1 large egg
1 cup sugar
1 cup self-rising flour, sifted
6 tablespoons butter, melted
1/2 teaspoons almond extract

- Preheat oven to 375 degrees.
- Place blackberries in a lightly greased two quart dish and sprinkle with lemon juice.
- In a separate bowl, stir together egg, sugar and flour until mixture resembles coarse meal.
- Stir in almond extract.
- Sprinkle the mixture over the fruit. Drizzle the melted butter over the cobbler.
- Bake for 35 minutes or until lightly browned and bubbly.
- Serve with ice cream or whipped cream.

Chicken and Dumplings

Chicken

1 whole fryer (3 to 4 pounds)
2 celery ribs, sliced
4 carrots, peeled and sliced
1 medium onion, diced
1 (14 ½ ounce) can chicken broth
1 ½ teaspoon salt
1 teaspoon pepper
water

• Place the fryer and vegetables in a dutch oven or a 6 to 8 quart pan. Add water to almost cover chicken.
• Cook over medium high until boiling and turn down to simmer. Cover and cook for 35 to 40 minutes.
• Remove chicken and vegetables from the broth. Remove skin and debone chicken. Chop chicken.
• Add the can of broth and enough water to the remaining liquid to cook dumplings.
• Bring to a boil and drop strips of dough (see below) one at a time into boiling broth until dumplings are cooked through about 15 minutes.
• Add chicken and vegetables back into broth with the dumplings.

And Dumplings

• My Big Ol' Southern Biscuit recipe (page 48)
• Roll dough out to a large rectangle about 1/8 inch thickness.
• Using a sharp knife, make strips 1 inch wide. Cut strips in half.
• Drop strips into boiling broth until cooked through about 15 minutes.
• Serve hot in soup bowl.

Chicken and Dumplings

My family made this recipe often in the winter because it is comfort. While growing up Mama would serve over a piece of white sandwich bread.

Today I present chicken and dumplings in a large soup bowl. This is Blake's favorite though he prefers Mama's over mine. Same recipe, go figure.

Alton had never eaten homemade dumplings until we married. He only knew of Sweet Sue and certainly that is not comparable to those made in a home kitchen.

Sweet Potato Pancakes

Charleston, South Carolina became a second home to me early in my marriage to Alton. From Nashville, our trips there rolled into the dreamy routine of driving the Isle of Palms Connector Bridge to the islands, walking the beaches of Sullivan Island, eating at our favorite restaurants and attending many of the downtown churches.

I am not proud of this, but during high tourist times, we sought a church based on the earliest service to let out; that way we could beat the crush to Sunday brunch.

In search of such timing, we discovered St Michael's Anglican Church and it began even earlier than we realized. As we opened the massive doors, we found ourselves immediately the center of attention because the sermon had already begun. No one was in the mood to make way for late-comers.

We headed for the one empty pew at the front of the sanctuary. Coming respectively from Presbyterian and Methodist backgrounds, Alton and I had no idea to the protocol of a gated pew. After struggling multiple times to open Pew #43, a parishioner stated "That's George's pew!"

Clueless, we continued our plight with the gate opening until she screeched, "That is George Washington's pew and no one is allowed to sit there!"

Since the entire congregation was focused on our every move and the sermon had stopped, we did what George Washington never did; we retreated. Our only consolation was to go to Joseph's Restaurant for sweet potato pancakes and jazz.

Recipe on next page

Sweet Potato Pancakes

1/2 cup sweet potato, mashed (1 medium sweet potato)
1/2 teaspoon cinnamon
1 tablespoon brown sugar
1 tablespoon butter
2 cups Bisquick
2 tablespoons sugar
1 teaspoon baking powder
1 teaspoon baking soda
1 egg, beaten
3/4 cup whole milk
2 tablespoon vegetable oil
1 teaspoon vanilla extract

- In a small bowl, add 1/2 cup mashed sweet potato, cinnamon, brown sugar and butter; mix well and set aside.
- In a large bowl, add baking mix, sugar, baking powder, baking soda, milk, oil, egg, vanilla and mashed sweet potato mixture.
- Stir just until moistened, the batter will be slightly lumpy. Over mixing results in tough pancakes.
- Using large stainless steel scoop, drop batter onto hot, lightly greased griddle or iron skillet. Cook over medium heat for 1 to 2 minutes. You will notice the bubbles forming; the edges will look slightly dry. Flip and cook for 1 to 2 more minutes or until golden brown.

Tip

To ensure the griddle or pan is hot, flick a drop of water on surface.
If water sputters and dances across the surface, it's the
right temperature. If it evaporates, it's too hot.

French Toast

3/4 cup whole milk
3/4 cup heavy cream (or half and half)
6 large eggs
1/4 cup sugar
1 teaspoon vanilla extract
1/2 teaspoon cinnamon
1/4 teaspoon salt
1 loaf of brioche bread, sliced 1 inch thick (approximately
   12 slices)
2 tablespoons butter
2 tablespoons oil
powdered sugar

- Preheat oven to 250 degrees.
- Add milk, cream, eggs, sugar, vanilla, cinnamon and salt in a 9x13x2 baking dish. Beat lightly.
- Add bread and turn to coat. Press down gently on bread with spatula until you feel it to start to soak up mixture. Let soak for 10 minutes.
- Flip bread and soak on other side another 5 to 10 minutes until saturated, but not soggy.
- Heat 1 tablespoon butter and 1 tablespoon oil in a large skillet over medium heat.
- Lift slices of bread from egg mixture letting excess drip off.
- Cook until golden brown and center of toast springs back when pressed, about 2 minutes per side.
- Even with a large skillet, the brioche loaf will require a repeat of the process to finish. Repeat process.
- Transfer toast to wire rack which is set inside rimmed baking sheet. Keep warm in oven while the remaining slices of bread are cooked.
- Sprinkle with powered sugar and serve with butter and warmed maple syrup.

French Toast

*T*he first time that I remember french toast is for a breakfast that my mama occasionally made using stale leftover white bread slices so as to not go to waste.

These days I love to make this dish for overnight visitors and friends using fresh brioche because of the flavorful outcome. I first discovered this recipe in *Southern Living*. The magazine has always been an important part of my life. I pour over every word, especially the recipes. Each issue is well worn, but safely kept for a revisit when researching recipes.

Recipe on previous page

Low Country Tomato Pie

There is nothing in this world like a good ol' homegrown tomato. During the summertimes of my life, I have enjoyed countless tomato recipes, but my first recollection of tomato pie came during a meal at a small restaurant in Mt. Pleasant, South Carolina.

From that time forward, I became determined to compose my own and began with my family biscuit recipe. Tomatoes and a biscuit, not bad at all.

My Big Ol' Southern Biscuit recipe (page 48)
4-6 tomatoes, peeled and sliced
10 fresh basil leaves, chopped
2 small cloves garlic, pressed
1 cup Monterey Jack cheese, grated
1 cup sharp cheddar cheese, grated
1 cup mayonnaise
salt and pepper
2 tablespoon flour

- Place tomatoes in colander and sprinkle with salt. Allow to drain for 10 to 15 minutes. Do not skip this step.
- Preheat oven to 350 degrees.
- Make the biscuit recipe to the point of rolling out to a 1/4 inch thickness.
- Place a 9-inch dinner plate over the rolled out dough. Using the plate as a pattern and a sharp knife, cut out the dough.
- Use a 9 inch pie plate and press the rolled out dough into bottom and sides.
- Flatten the top edge of the dough on the rim with tines of a fork.
- Prick the crust with the fork tines across the bottom to prevent rising and making bubbles. Par bake for 5 minutes.
- Sprinkle tomatoes with flour, salt and pepper. Layer tomatoes with basil inside the pie crust.
- Combine the grated cheeses, mayonnaise, and garlic together. Spread mixture on top of the tomatoes and seal to edges.
- Bake for 30 minutes or more until lightly browned.

Place baking sheet under pie to catch any excess oil or juice.

Sweet Milk Toast

*O*ur family enjoyed the results of this recipe as a meal in itself or for a quick dessert.

This recipe came from my Grandaddy's mother, Ma Johnson. My Grandaddy was the youngest of her ten children.

She taught her daughter-in-law, my Grandmommie, a great many skills like cooking, canning and preserving.

Here is a long lasting comfort recipe that is her legacy.

6 slices of white bread
2 cups milk
1 teaspoon vanilla
3/4 cup sugar

• Toast 6 slices of white bread, toasted on both sides
• Heat 2 cups sweet or whole milk.
• Add 1 teaspoon vanilla and 3/4 cup sugar in milk and stir.
• Pour hot milk over toasted bread.
• Enjoy immediately.

The recipe may be prepared in half or thirds.

Cinnamon Toast

When I was in the third grade, we moved from our country house across the field from Grandma and Papa Rose into Pulaski where people were on all sides of us. Our backdoor neighbors were the Barkstrom family from Michigan.

I became fast friends with their two girls, Beth and Dawn. We were inseparable and I loved eating at their house because they introduced me to foods that we did not eat like peanut butter on buttered toast for breakfast.

We never had anything like that, just the traditional breakfast of eggs, bacon, biscuits and gravy. The only thing that Mama ever made outside the usual was cinnamon toast. What a treat!

Sliced Bread
Cinnamon
Sugar
Butter

- Bring butter to room temperature.
- Spread butter over bread.
- Mix equal amounts of cinnamon and sugar in a bowl and place in a shaker.
- Sprinkle bread evenly with cinnamon/sugar mixture using a flour or sugar shaker.
- Place prepared bread on cookie sheet and toast until bubbly and toasted around the edges.

Strawberry Creme Puffs

Strawberry Creme Puffs

The first of every May, I look forward to those sweet little white flowers that turn into beautiful red, juicy strawberries, my favorite fruit in the whole wide world. Maybe it is because strawberries are members of the rose family and I am from the Rose family.

Every spring the Rose family from Pulaski loved to travel to our favorite patch in the neighboring town of Lawrenceburg to pick our heart's desire. Still today each May, I love nothing better than to call ahead to pick my own at Limoland in Giles County.

Afterwards with a basketful, I head back to my Nashville kitchen with the perfect goods for this treasured combo, a more recent version of strawberry shortcake.

Strawberries

1 quart strawberries
1/2 cup sugar

• Wash berries in colander and turn out on paper towels to dry. Hull strawberries.
• Slice each strawberry into thin slices. Pour sugar over to macerate, about 30 minutes.

Creme Puffs

1 cup water
1/2 cup unsalted butter
1 cup all-purpose flour
4 eggs

Continued next page

Strawberry Creme Puffs (con't)

- Preheat oven to 400 degrees.
- Heat water and butter to a boil in a 4 quart sauce pan.
- Stir in flour as it quickly becomes a ball. Remove from the heat.
- One at a time, stir in each egg with a fork, until the mixture is well blended and resembles dough.
- Drop by teaspoonfuls onto a parchment lined baking sheet.
- Bake for 25 minutes or until light golden brown.
- Remove from oven and cool for about 10 minutes. Prepare whipped cream while the creme puffs cool.
- To prepare, split creme puff and place a tablespoon of strawberries inside and spilling outside, top with whipped cream. Place a sprig of mint on top to serve.

Whipped Cream

> **1 cup whipping cream**
> **2 tablespoons powdered sugar**
> **1/2 teaspoon Grand Mariner or vanilla extract**

- Ahead of time, place mixing bowl and beaters in the freezer to chill for at least 10 minutes.
- Place whipping cream in bowl and beat for 2 minutes, add sugar and flavoring and beat until stiff peak form.

Spreads & Gravies

A warm biscuit deserves hot blackberry jam......

Every year around the 4th of July was blackberry picking time. My Granddadddy would go up the road to Uncle Willie and Aunt Effie Johnson's farm and bush hog a path to the best blackberry patch in Giles County.

We would arm ourselves with long sleeves and long pants with belts to keep the chiggers, mosquitoes and copperhead snakes from biting us, load onto the back of his pickup truck and head out to the fresh cut path.

Grandaddy was the master of blackberry picking. Our tools were handled buckets which were hooked on to our belts allowing us to pick freely with both hands. Granddaddy would check our buckets occasionally to make sure we were not goofing off. It was a challenge to see who could fill their bucket first and the larger berries would do the job faster!

Upon returning home, everything was turned into Grandmommie who gave instructions for "putting up the berries." Carefully washed and drained, the juicy berries found their way into one cup frozen portions for hot jam. Other berries were made into blackberry jelly through canning.

We looked forward to the blackberry yumminess that would top biscuits, cornbread, dumplings, ice cream and particularly the ugly biscuit (page 49) for the months to come.

1 cup fresh or frozen blackberries
1 cup sugar

- Place the blackberries and sugar in a small pan on top of the stove at medium heat. Turn to simmer, stirring occasionally with a spoon for about 20 minutes.
- This combination must never boil. The jam will be thin, but will thicken over time.
- Use a spoon to skim off any foam that appears. Transfer the jam to a jar and let cool completely. Refrigerate if not using immediately.

Country Ham Spread

*E*very workday as I open the Winery at Belle Meade Plantation, I am struck by the beauty of the adjoining building, The Ham House. This three story structure is considered to be the largest brick smokehouse in the South. During Belle Meade's heyday of entertaining business titans, presidents, dignitaries and horsemen of the nineteenth century, as many as 60 hogs would be slaughtered at one time and the entire smokehouse would be filled to capacity with only hams and slabs of bacon.

The likes of Davy Crockett, Andrew Jackson, Presidents Polk, Johnson, Taft and Roosevelt all enjoyed the salty, hickory smoked hams from the smokehouse in all its forms, sliced whole ham, center cuts and fillers for biscuits, shaved ham and of course, ham spread.

The first time I ever tasted Country Ham Spread was at a delicious "welcome to Belle Meade party" held in our honor by Roberta Lochte-Jones. She served cocktails with tea biscuits and country ham spread.

In Nashville, a party is not a party without dime-sized country ham biscuits and cheese straws to accompany cocktails. This may not be as true as it certainly once was, but it remains a tradition in our house.

1 ½ cups center cut slices country ham
2 tablespoons spicy or honey mustard
1 teaspoon chopped onion

- Heat the proper size iron skillet to accommodate the pieces. Place slices into skillet and heat for 2 minutes and then turn to cook on the other side.
- Drizzle 2 tablespoons of coca-cola and cook an additional 2 minutes.
- Remove from skillet immediately.
- Place ingredients into food processor and chop finely. Measure 1 ½ cups and return to food processor. Add mustard and onion and pulse until a spreadable consistency.
- Serve on bite sized biscuits.

Red Eye Gravy

Granddaddy told this story of his youth. He was sickly, being the youngest, he caught everything that his brothers and sisters had such as chicken pox, measles, mumps and whooping cough.

His mother Ma Johnson would fix him broken pieces of biscuits in sweetened coffee with milk to heal all. She would pull hot ashes and red-hot coals to the front of the fireplace and level them out in order to place an iron skillet on them and heat a big ol' biscuit with homemade butter on top.

He often recalled what good kitchen memories those were.

country ham slices
1/2 cup black coffee

• After frying country ham, remove from skillet.
• To the drippings left in the skillet, add hot black coffee.
• Scrape the bottom and sides of the skillet to get all the ham particles.
• Bring to a boil and serve hot over a warm biscuit.
• This is a thin gravy. Use biscuit to sop up the gravy and serve with a
 side of grits.

Sweet Milk Gravy

My family loved the taste of sweet milk gravy on our biscuits. Often in the wintertime, we would have a quick supper of biscuits and minute steaks with gravy ladled all over. Grandmommie and Grandaddy had biscuits and sweet milk gravy every morning.

Sweet milk gravy can be nuanced. If serving bacon, sausage or minute steaks, the drippings can be used to make "a more seasoned gravy". Granddaddy whipped Karo Syrup and butter together to serve over his biscuit for "dessert."

Recipie on next page

Sweet Milk Gravy

3 tablespoons cooking oil
3 tablespoons self-rising flour, sifted
1 ½ cup whole milk
pepper

- Heat large cast iron skillet to a medium-high heat.
- Add oil or drippings and then sift flour directly into the pan. Stir constantly with whisk until smooth and begins to thicken and lightly brown. Keep stirring as the milk is gradually added. Cook on medium-high heat until the gravy begins to bubble.
- Should the gravy become too thick, add a small amount of milk or warm water until thinned. Season with pepper. We never used any other seasonings including salt, just pepper, because we preferred the sweet milk taste to stand on its own.

The term sweet milk is an ol' timey reference used to differentiate whole milk (sweet) and buttermilk (sour).

A life path of affection for the kitchen and its mysteries opened for me by chance in the early 1990s. With a demanding position in banking, I longed to spend more time with my two little boys while earning an income.

I was invited to a Pampered Chef Party by my sister-in-law and liked what I saw. Similar to the Tupperware parties of yore, The Pampered Chef is a network marketing company that promotes kitchen tools and recipes by hosting in-home parties. I signed up.

The boys were thrilled with the decision and I soon discovered my sales efforts would be rewarded with a trip to Disney World for the entire family. The founder and CEO of The Pampered Chef Doris Christopher created a fair shake for me as she had for herself when she started the company (it was so well run that it was eventually purchased by Warren Buffett of Berkshire Hathaway).

My first television appearance as a chef on WSMV channel 4.

I began to offer cooking demonstrations all over Tennessee and North Alabama. I built a team of fifty consultants by sharing my story. Most became lifelong friends. I was invited to speak to 200 of my peers. That led to regular speaking engagements at the national conference for years to come.

With assurances from Doris and the Pampered Chef home office staff, I began to knock it out of the park becoming a top seller in the nation and number one in Tennessee. Even as the business grew to 40,000 consultants, opportunities for prosperity were everywhere. I will always remember Doris's encouraging words and sincere concerns for my family.

Throughout I helped my boys with their homework, took them to practice or Boy Scouts and then left a meal in the oven for supper. Their Dad would see them to bed as I often worked until ten o'clock. But to be sure, before school the next morning, My Big Ol' Southern Biscuits (see page 48) would always be ready for breakfast.

I learned that all things are possible. That spirit moves with me while I teach lessons on how to bake and cook in my current position as Manager of Food and Spirits at The Belle Meade Plantation in Nashville, Tennessee. And to this day before a class, I lean upon Philippians 4:13, "I can do all things through Christ who strengthens me" with an added blessing for everyone who has given me the chance to share the things in life that have brought me to a full table.

Chocolate Gravy

When my Daddy was a young boy he would gather eggs for my Grandma Rose. Often she would allow him to sell the extra eggs he would gather for the peddler who would come to the house. Another exchange made with the peddler would be the purchase of cocoa powder that she used to make this chocolate gravy.

6 tablespoons unsalted butter
1/4 cup self-rising flour
1/4 cup unsweetened cocoa powder
1 cup sugar
2 cups whole milk
1/2 teaspoon vanilla extract

• Melt butter over medium heat in a 12 inch cast iron skillet.
• Whisk together flour, cocoa powder and sugar in a small bowl. Whisk flour mixture into melted butter until the flour mixture is moist.
• Slowly whisk in milk and continue to cook, whisking constantly, until the chocolate gravy has thickened to the consistency of a gravy or thin pudding.
• Remove pan from heat and stir in vanilla.
• Serve warm with hot buttered biscuits.

Island Cheese Spread

This is a Bahamian version of Southern pimento cheese. Every winter, Alton and I stay several weeks in the Bahamas. Our greatest joy while there is to dine with newfound friends.

On one such occasion, a neighbor told me about this famous Hope Town spread. This can be served on biscuits, crackers or rolls. Children love it on sandwich bread.

> **3 cups cheddar cheese, shredded**
> **8 ounces cream cheese**
> **8 ounces sour cream**
> **3 tablespoon onion, minced**
> **3 tablespoons green pepper, minced**
> **3 shots of hot sauce**
> **1/8 teaspoon salt**

- Mix it all together.
- Chill and serve.

Honey Butter

2 tablespoons unsalted butter, melted
2 tablespoons honey

• Melt 2 tablespoons butter on stovetop or in microwave and then stir in
  2 tablespoons honey.

Pecan Honey Butter

*S*everal years ago, Alton, the boys and I visited Ireland. Our first stop
was The Butter Museum in Cork. Butter lovers that we are, we appreciated
the history of production and sales and the tour around the original butter
market.

1/2 cup butter, softened
1/2 cup confectioner's sugar
1/2 cup honey
1/4 cup chopped pecans, toasted

• In a medium mixing bowl, combine butter, sugar and honey. Beat until
  light and fluffy.
• Stir in pecan pieces.
• Form into log or place into butter mold and refrigerate up to 2 weeks.
  Serve over pancakes, waffles, biscuits or toast.

*But butter and pecans — too much of a good thing, you say? What could be better on a
Southern butter plate than the addition of this beautiful blend?*

Tip

To toast pecans: Preheat oven to 350 degrees.
Place chopped pecans on baking sheet and toast for
5 minutes or until they become aromatic.

Acknowledgments

This book has been an emotional rollercoaster ride and would not have been possible without the support of so many.

First and foremost, to my family for their endless support and love. Thank you for believing in me. To my husband, **Alton**, for the many trips to the grocery when I would forget something; number one taste-tester, biggest cheerleader, wagging dishes and props around, setting scenes, inspiration and unending love. I could not have done it without you.

To my son **Blake**, for your love and encouraging words daily. This book is written as a tribute to our families and that you will never forget from whence you came.

To our son, **Robert**, for always being a willing taster and cheerleader.

To **Mama** and **Daddy**, for teaching me to work hard and never give up.

To my friend and editor, **Roben Mounger**, for your food knowledge, excellent writing skills, testing and re-testing recipes, unending emails and texts — your nudge and encouragement kept me going.

To **Neil White** and the team at **The Nautilus Publishing Company**. What a joy it has been to work with such a professional group of folks. Your patience was unbelievable — when you would say, "take a break and the inspiration will come" — you were right! You are such a talented individual. Thank you for believing in the project and that I could do this.

To my photographer, **Michael Gomez**, what a pro! Your talent, techniques, creativity and skills brought my food story to life. Every photograph is beyond belief.

To your assistant, **Amanda Harrison**, who could not have been more helpful with every shot.

To my food stylist, **Amanda Alberto**, what a keen eye you have for food. I was blown away when you arrived with your car full of props and everything that we might have needed. You strapped on your work apron and away you went without even a word from me.

To my cousin, **Mimi Heldman**, for your time and talent.

To my long-time friend, **Carolyn Rains**, as a great recipe tester.

To **Belle Meade Plantation and Winery staff** for putting up with the photo shoots and allowing me to complete this project.

To my entire team a great big heartfelt "thank you."

How grateful I am to all!!